ALONG THE WAY

Poems

JABULANI MZINYATHI

Mwanaka Media and Publishing Pvt Ltd,
Chitungwiza Zimbabwe
*
Creativity, Wisdom and Beauty

Publisher: *Mmap*
Mwanaka Media and Publishing Pvt Ltd
24 Svosve Road, Zengeza 1
Chitungwiza Zimbabwe
mwanaka@yahoo.com
mwanaka13@gmail.com
https://www.mmapublishing.org
www.africanbookscollective.com/publishers/mwanaka-media-and-publishing
https://facebook.com/MwanakaMediaAndPublishing/

Distributed in and outside N. America by African Books Collective
orders@africanbookscollective.com
www.africanbookscollective.com

ISBN: 978-1-77931-469-7
EAN: 9781779314697

DISCLAIMER
All views expressed in this publication are those of the author and
do not necessarily reflect the views of *Mmap*.

DEDICATION

This work is dedicated to all the editors of the various magazines that gave space to the various poems. Some of them have passed on. Others are still alive. In the same breath I speak of people like Onesimo Makani Kabweza, Tichaona Mukuku, Donatas Bonde, Zerubabel Mudzingwa, John Vekris, Percy Makombe and many others that I may not readily remember. My thanks also to publications like *Moto, Social Change, Mahogany, Compost* [USA] and ezines like *OneGhanaOneVoice*. My hearty thanks to *Mbizo Chirasha* and *Tendai Rinos Mwanaka* who have rekindled my interest in getting these works out there. Jah guide and protect I and I.

Contents

AUTHOR'S NOTE

This is a project that I have been thinking about for a very long time. I refer here to the period 1992 to date. It is made up largely of my poems published by **publications such as** *Moto magazine* and *Social Change* during the long and tortuous Mugabe era. Where dates are remembered, these have been indicated just below the specific poems. In terms of writing, these poems stem from the formative years. Then like now I was a budding writer. Does a writer ever fully bloom? I doubt that. For that reason I remain a budding writer.

The poems touch on a variety of themes or subjects. Of course the dominant issue is a rejection of the excesses of the Mugabe regime. I loathed that shitstem [shit system]. I always believed that it would fall. Indeed it fell. Not quite vanquished! I always felt deep inside me that I would live to see it humiliated and that the man at the helm would die in exile. He did though not in the manner I had envisioned. To a large extent the poems were or are somewhat prophetic. Evil systems always crumble.

The Mugabe system created heroes out of all kinds of shady characters. **They** lie at the heroes acre. Ironically Mugabe himself does not lie buried at that monument. In one of the poems selected to be part of this collection I talk of a monument that may be overgrown with weeds. We will take stock and see that some so-called heroes are actually villains! That place is therefore a somewhat defiled place. Men like Lookout Masuku, Ndabaningi Sithole were left out. Now if those are not heroes then who is? Dumiso Dabengwa who also does not lie at the so- called heroes acre refused to have opportunists preside at his funeral and tell lies. The story of our country is yet to be written.

A lie often repeated will never be the truth. It will never stand the test of time.

These poems have not been thematically arranged as happened in my collections *Under The Steel Yoke* and *Righteous Indignation*. That decision has been deliberately taken. Life is not patterned. These poems are a microcosm of the life lived under Robert Mugabe. The country was and still is one psychiatric ward where the patients masquerading as doctors administer drugs with tragic consequences. The poems though dealing with bleak subjects have an undercurrent of hope. They capture the essence of my people.

The story of Robert Mugabe is a long one. That is so because he had created a personality cult. He was the god. His worshippers believed he was not a mere mortal but the truth is now here. He lies somewhere in his grave vanquished. Robert Mugabe believed he was the best thing that ever happened to Zimbabwe. Some of us know that he was just a power hungry monster. Many of the poems in this collection speak to his misrule. Anyone is free, is to hold their own views. That is what democracy is basically about. These poems express my views about that era.

Another theme that received attention is the condemnation of political violence. Political violence has bedeviled this nation from the time Mugabe assumed power. The violence is still here with us. The levels of political intolerance are still nauseating. The core of the architects of violence is still here. Mugabe bragged about degrees in violence. Some of the degreed ones are still around and their end will surely come. The myth of invincibility will be shattered.

One of the themes that has preoccupied me is the warped form of Christianity that treats black people as sin. I have also been dealing with apostasy. Further another theme that gives me sleepless nights is how spirit mediums were consulted during the liberation struggle and were vilified and dumped after independence. There were even attempts to call Zimbabwe a Christian country by some opportunists that were hiding in America, Britain and other places when the war of liberation raged on guided by the spirits now reviled and termed evil. That is a lot of crap.

There are many themes that the poems, spanning over two decades, tackle. Many lives were lost as desperate Zimbabweans tried to illegally cross into South Africa in search of greener pastures. Many ended up in the bellies of man eating crocodiles in the Limpopo River. Many are still drowning while others become crocodiles' food. Their restless spirits must find peace. The people of Zimbabwe must find rest. The master-servant relationship has been replaced by the povo-shef relationship. The poem entitled 'Celebration Time' is about that. 'We' and 'Them' has reached levels that were inconceivable at independence when we were so filled with hope which turned out to be just empty euphoria. The poet still speaks today. This collection speaks to today and tomorrow while drawing from the lessons of the past. What is it that is past?

An Indictment

An indictment for pseudo-revolutionaries
Profaning the sacrosanct
Attempting vainly to uproot our struggle
Steadfast in our way we remain
What is fundamental they trivialise
The guardian spirits are forgotten
Ask the true freedom fighters
Warped Christianity now takes centre stage
 No longer invoked are ancestral spirits
The errant shall get a beating
The struggle now a personal possession
A dangerous personality cult is propagated
In deprivation and depravation masses wallow
In extreme bewilderment they wallow
The system has become dirt clogged
The detergent is here with us all the time
Those ideals that gave rise to the struggle

[13.12.04]

The Inevitable End

You never took heed
No permanent friends
Only those permanent interests
You did not listen to this
Whosoever diggeth a pit shall fall in it
You never wanted to learn those lessons
You got too sloshed by power
In the end the monsters gobble their makers
Ask those that pave way for dictators
Ask those that created Frankenstein
Your erudition has gone to waste
It was branded evil genius
Now a spider trapped in its own web
Those draconian pieces of legislation
The monster you made shall feast on you
The disciples of Machiavelli are at it
Do they merciless deserve mercy

[20.12.04]

2

The Looming Struggle

As you stampeded for prime land
You did not remotely take heed of that voice
Of the ant voice you never took heed
On unimaginable greed you lived
As you rode on the backs of the landless
Vociferously you shouted your slogans
The racial landholding was the issue
The barren lands you did not decongest
Don't say that I did not warn you
The storm of righteous indignation was rising
The pertinent questions were being asked
The black petit bourgeoisie was taking over
Taking over from the white kleptomaniacs
Nothing changed but the landlord's colour
The tell-tale signs were not missing
That righteous struggle you shall demonise
When the down trodden take up arms

[28.12.04]

Bubble Burst

The soap bubble burst
The certainty of inevitability
Like a village imp you acted
Taking village wells like a piss pot
Humility you struck with a back hander
The devil's guest you were
Ended up becoming the devil's meal
What else did you anticipate?
What magic wand can you now wave?
A nonentity you now are
Will your past incisive works redeem you?
Were you a midwife of a new dispensation?

[28.12.04]

Through The Veil

In the name of a global village
Sing the still sad song of self-denigration
Reap the rewards of foolishness
Throw out the baby with the bath water
The European model is the ideal
Those green backs are blood stained
Stained with our innocent blood
The pound sterling is steeped in our sweat
From stolen gold deriving strength
See the protracted concerted vicious assault
This Eurocentric perspective is modernity
Afrocentric perceptions are the devil incarnate
Sing fervently the songs of self-denigration
Those thought tracks are ineradicable
There is this timeless yearning for liberty

[03.02.05]

Warrior Spirit

Cannot hold back any longer
That vibrant warrior spirit
In the face of merciless adversaries
Cannot restrain the soul rebel
That pretended conformity shattered
That meekness mistaken for weakness
Listen that fight is definitely on
That warrior poet delivers mortal blows
Forever true to those ways of old
That blood courses through my veins
I can never be a brand new man
Stand in the way of this colossus
That fight is on now and forever

[05.03.05]

Dangerous Qualification

The rumblings of schizophrenia
Slapping nationalism is the face
Poisoning posterity's wells
Clinging to warped tribal ideas
A negation of that bitter struggle
Profaning that sacrosanct blood
Derailing those ideals of old
We are citizens of the world
Your superiority is ill clad inferiority
The dangerous sycophants get the crumbs
Their irrelevance is now at hand
You have been weighed in the balance
You have now been found wanting
A discordant voice among crooners

[21.03.05]

Broken

Though limbs be broken
And bad words spoken
That will is not dented
It was so in the past
So shall it be now and tomorrow
That primeval beast roars
It shall be shredded
The people's will reigns supreme

[22.03.03]

After A long Night

And the doves begin to coo
That is the breaking of dawn
Myriad chirping of birds
Mirthfully darting from tree to tree

Those eerie moments are gone
That unnerving hooting of owls
The ominous hyena laughs
The death and destruction lurking

[23.03.03]

To Hope

Then the foe appears formidable at times
That fight you almost give up
But then freedom is an ontological vocation
There is no succulence in being a victim
Then you drink from the wells of the past
There is the cool fountain of inspiration
That story of David and Goliath
That of Samson and the Philistines
You draw on the exploits of Moses
You delve then into our folklore
The realization that king owl has no horns
And that the elephant was felled by an ant
Crush now the blood sucking lice
This time is not for despair

[28.03.03]

Of Light And Darkness

What a profanation
Men of the cloth
By their balls, held
In the claws of manipulation
At the devil's throne
Drinking human blood
A god ordained order
Fanning fiery fires of strife
What a profanation
Men of the cloth
Choosing to sing songs of praise
Aiding and abetting iniquities
Light shall drive away this darkness
Mirthfully the children shall play
This story cannot be obliterated

[20.01.02]

The Defilement

These lines
The exhumation of ideals
Buried under mounds of lies
That blood
Defiled by opportunists
It boils in anger
Those bones
They shall arise
That great prophetess said it
'Mapfupa angu achamuka'
It was said it shall be done
For in the beginning was the word
Wiping off this defilement
These lines
(Mapfupa angu achamuka is chiShona meaning my bones will rise)

[07.03.02]

In A Rut

With bated breath
With much trepidation
An avalanche of questions
A turbulent future looms
Gloomily stuck in this rut

Tough Choices Again

The hunger and drought
The thick squalor
The glamour and glitter
Across the Limpopo
Man eating crocodiles
Vicious big jawed hippos
The looming drowning
This social, economic, political malaise
Tough choices, ahead
There, to face xenophobia
Give me ignorance
This knowledge hurts
Forces of retrogression lead
Perpetuating the fragmentation

[21.05.02]

Exorcism

Lunacy grabs the throats
Muffling dissenting voices
Enemies are then imagined
Patriots labelled dissidents

Lunacy holds sway
Everywhere the eavesdropping
Despots fear the people
Repression cannot last forever

Here lunacy is normalcy
The deifying of mere mortals
See the futility of it all
Shit and piss on their holiness

[21.05.02]

Emancipation

To the Promised Land
That is where we want to go
Dropping the shackles and chains
We can't bear the pains

Pharaoh, let my people go
For too long we have been captives
We want to sing freedom songs now
Masters of our destiny, we are

To the Promised Land
That is where we want to be
There, to be like sand on the sea shore
There, to fulfill our creator's plan

Your defiled wells, we don't want
Keep your caustic milk and honey
Sing songs of victory, we shall
Now we sing songs of redemption

[27.10.02]

Unveiling

Take off the lid
That cauldron
The wizard's broth
This is the exorcism
That counterfeit history
The mounds of lies
The profaning of life
The profound lessons
King owl has no horns
That time is nigh
Heal the wounds now

[28.07.02]

Feather In A Whirlwind

This maddening turbulence
This swirling whirlpool
Feather in the whirlwind
Deranging upheavals trap
I seek salvation now
The obliteration of demonic conditions
This thick wintry darkness
How to retain sanity
These tears ease the pain
In this thick labyrinth
The Minotaur pursuing me

[30.07.02]

Drunk

You got inebriated
That intoxicant
Father, I shudder
Shudder to call you that
You got inebriated
Children you brutalized
Became very drunk
Children went hungry
Homeless and insane
Still you were drunk
The home now broken
Still you are sloshed
Children you drive away
Where is the future?
Where is your pride?
When children roam the streets
Begging, begging profusely
What mindless rage seized you?

[01.08.02]

Longing

When shall we sit?
Coolness of a shade
Garden with birds of all plumage
When shall we sit?
Eagerly taking in
The sweet fragrances
The uplifting of our souls
The tapestry of music
Water falling down rocks
When shall we sit?
Cool embrace of tranquility
When shall we bask?
The sunshine of truth and justice
Iniquities off our shoulders
When shall we sit?
Say it was just a rough patch
Learn the great lessons of love

Birth Pangs

Desperation and lunacy
Clad in jackboots
Despotic perceptions
Wielded thought crushing batons
O, loaded rifles too
The bruised revellers,
Revellers dazed out of their wits
Life rendered cheap
The future in the womb
These are the birth pangs
Don't fertilise the seeds of despondency
Sing that song of hope
None, none but ourselves
Those scars are the badges
The badges of liberation
The story shall be told
The future in the womb
These are the birth pangs

[03.08.02]

The Shame Of It

Persecution pervades the nostrils
Society catches the disease
See the graves
See the fear everywhere
There are the terrorists

Voice Of Progress

For the miserable crumbs
Falling from the high tables
Of the banqueting ghosts
Drunk on sweat, tears and blood
For the false consciousness
That nonsense about shared goals
A false sense of belonging
Perpetuating the shit system
They don't flinch at all
Maggot-like spies and informers
See the decimation of dissent
Silencing the voices of progress

[27.08.02]

Between Word and Deed

It is all bark
There is no bite
It is just thunder
Without the lightning
Empty rhetoric
That path is littered
Corpses of deserted plans
Now we know the truth
See the deep chasm
Between word and deed
Grand plans with no fruits
There on the architect's board
The reverberations of rhetoric
The rumblings in our stomachs

[05.09.02]

Discordant voice

You sing out of tune
Yet my voice, you call discordant
You pollute my ear drums
With your discordant voice
Society is the choir master
Your days are numbered

[05.09.02]

Soul Seekers

Soul seekers
In the wake of this cataclysm
Preaching apostasy
My soul is not for sale
Take your salvation elsewhere
The ways of my ancestors beckon
Keep your unsolicited advice
Soul seekers

[29.10.04]

Artist

The poems, short stories
Publications galore
The abundance of funds
Now the spotlight
Death has struck

Those songs
The very little airplay
Disc jockeys fall over each other
Now the abundance of air play
Death has struck

The sculptures, paintings
Now collectors' items
The exhibitions
All those rave reviews
The artist takes centre stage

This is the conundrum
The artist must die
Die in order to live
That is the fullness of life
Death has struck

[09.11.04]

27

Bumper Harvests

If you don't see the bumper harvests
On the minister's two chins
If you don't see the bumper harvests
Right there on the television screens
There in the vibrant radio jingles
Then you sow seeds of despondency
Talking of those children with distended stomachs
Sparsely growing tufts of brownish hair
And almost visible rib cages
A threat to national security, you are
Those so-called statistics on malnutrition deaths
Those are the works of your western funders
We see through the evil hidden hand

[24.11.04]

The Refinery

The acrid smell
Of burning human flesh
The petrol fumes
Aftermath of petrol bombs
The stench of rotting flesh
Maggot infested corpses
There in those shallow graves
Victims of gross intolerance
Victims of warped thinking

Give us political detainees
From behind prison walls
Let us have a new dispensation
From behind prison walls
And the solitary confinement
Graduates should emerge
Evaluating that revolution

Blinding torrents of intolerance
Narcissus, your bigotry
Your attempts to defy gravity
That is your inevitable demise
No one shall sound the last post
No one shall sing the dirges
But there still is a chance

[08.12.04]

Under The Steel Yoke

The wiry and ghoulish
The hand of despondency
This unfortunate present
The condemned future
Tightly in its steel fingers grip
The warped ideas
Chaining the present and the future
In the brimming prisons of despair
Crest fallen
Led by stale ideas
Pummeled by vicious propaganda
Self-proclaimed saviours
Shamelessly clipping our wings
Desirous of making us automatons
This is the stone the builder refused
That is now the head cornerstone

[Moto October 2006 composed 10.11.99]

Emperor In The Nude

Now it dawns on the emperor
That he has no clothes on
That he is the last to know it
The babes and the suckling know it
The shame of it sticks out
Just like a sore thumb it sticks out
The nudity leaves and indelible mark
It used to be said in hushed tones
Now hear the echoes in the mountains and hills
Hear the words in valleys and plains
Time is the greatest master
Sing these songs of hope
In hope is the sweetness of tomorrow

[Moto September 2003]

Condemned

Once exalted
Now reviled and rejected
Deep down in the dust
Your wretched name
An epitome of soullessness
Your welcome you overstayed
Prayers to the devil you said
The innocent blood you drank
That orgy of senseless killings
Those indelible bitter scars
The castration of the nation
The sacrosanct you profaned
Limbs, lives senselessly lost
Machiavellian machinations manifested
Drown the narcissus drown
That myth of invincibility now shattered
Rot now wicked miscreant rot
Down in the maggot infested dungeon

[Moto May 2004 composed 12.10.03]

To Fela Anikulapo Ransome Kuti

Fela Anikulapo Kuti
What scathing attack
What scorpion sting
For your blundering compatriot
Tell me Fela, tell me
What would you say?
About this warped Pan Africanism
Condoning black on black violence
Seeing not the rut we are in
Tell me Fela, tell me

[Moto Magazine February 2004 composed 27.02.03]

33

Not Heeded

And when the artist speaks
Through deft brush strokes
On the canvas
Through the chipping chisel
On the marble, soapstone
Through the prancing lines
The prancing lines of bitter-sweet poetry
That soothsayer I hear
Caesar beware the ides of March
Let those that have ears hear

[Moto Magazine November 2001]

Instant Riches

Bits of betting cards
Strewn on the floor
Like confetti
Bits of fractured dreams
Furrowed faces frustration laden
Shattered dreams everywhere
Placing bet upon bet
Hoping, hoping, hoping
Immersed in expectancy

[Moto Magazine November 2001]

That Man-Yogi Guvheya Guvheya Nyamunderu

Austerity
Simplicity
Bohemianism , or is it
Waves of doubt engulf these thoughts
Rejection of materialism
Lustrous spiritualism
Labels piling up
Not one apposite
Their songs rejecting
Maybe just standing aloof
Lives touching
Lasting impressions etching
Monuments erecting
Shattering conservatism
Exuding brilliance
Touching souls
Illuminating the dark recesses
Deluge upon deluge of questions
Embracing humanity in its entirety
Writer? Philosopher? Poet?
Unraveled mystery
Anointed by the gods
A harbinger of hope
A soothsayer
Fitting not into pigeon hole
What is taken for granted, subverting
Not a conscious effort

Life undefiled
Freely flowing
That man
Forever in timelessness
Not a subject for empty eulogies
Though life be refined in death
That man
Basking in the sunshine of immortality
A chronicle of his life not praise
A dissertation on that man
That man

(Moto June 2001)

Yet Another Gap

While you lived
You were a foe
To be persecuted at every turn
Reviled and rejected
For lighting the fire that warmed them
The fire they claim to have lit
Having elbowed you away
You were demonized
For they feared the truth
For your blood they bayed
When their opportunism you exposed
In your death you haunt them
Haunting them more than when you lived
That which they now see
You had long seen and tried to correct

Enjoying the sound of their voices
They chose not to listen
Haunt them in their committees
Their hypocrisy we see
Like trees that bear no fruit
They shall be cut and burnt
Fools standing lip deep in water
See their parched throats
The warping of your story
That we shall not allow
They shall be weighed in the balance

They shall be found wanting
Shameless masters of double speak
Look at their monuments
The weeds shall choke them
For they are like a house built on the sand
You, the stone the builder refused
The head-corner stone you shall be
The story not yet told
This nation shall drink
At the well you dug
Together with others they choose to forget
The fullness of life is in your death
It is always so with the resilient

[Moto March 2001.Composed 12.12.2000 in honour of Rev
Ndabaningi Sithole. He played his part in our liberation but was a
victim of a coup back then!]

What Cheek

Thinking is a luxury
Don't engage in it
Follow the leader
Question not his blindness
Just toe the line
Deviate at your peril
Read not so called independent papers
Read only officially sanctioned materials
There wisdom is in abundance
There the truth is
Forget about official censorship
Unofficial censorship rules
The rule of law my foot
Distance yourself from luxuries
Confine to faculty corridors
Those debates on the rule of law
Ask not any questions
[Moto February 2001]

This Time

Of revolution
Fiery fires
Fanned
Dawning
The new dispensation

Shackles and chains
Truncheons
Batons
Live ammunition
The kicks of a dying horse

This time, no holding back
Those that cannot change
Shall surely bend
That is the inevitable end

[Moto February 2001]

Revelation Time

To snuff out lives
Of those with different views
Aiwa handidi

To have innocent blood
On these hands
Aiwa handidi

To drag home a fiery
Fiery avenging spirit
Aiwa handidi

To be a pawn
In these games of poly tricks
Aiwa handidi

To wine and dine
With the angel Lucifer
Aiwa handidi

To embrace a false sense
A false sense of superiority
Aiwa handidi

To violate the sanctity of life
Aiwa handidi

To be an automaton
Aiwa handidi

A house built upon a rock
That is what I choose to be
This is introspection time

[*Aiwa handidi*- No, I do not want. Moto June 2000]

Cryptic Poetry

There is a poet
Embedded in every prophet

Taste the caustic poetry
Issuing from mounds of poverty

See the smooth poetry
Spun like pottery on the potter's wheel

The prancing lines of potent poetry
The poet's intellectual property

[Moto February 2000]

To All Thinkers

Lightning in the testicles
Bomb blasts in the skull
Thunder claps in the ears
Violent throbs in the flesh
Aftermaths of demons' ways

Indifference is a transgression
An unforgivable transgression

On you the maggots will feed
Loud and clear shout it
The sanctity of our liberty
That web of fear obliterate

Indifference is a transgression
An unforgivable transgression

[To Mark Chavhunduka Moto October 1999]

For The Umpteenth Time

The poets have spoken

'Inglan is a bitch fe true'
The baritone of Linton Kwesi Johnson

'It no good to live in a whiteman's country too long'
The incisive voice of Mutabaruka

'You think you are in heaven
But you are living in hell'
The prophetic Bob Marley wails

Now you live in slime and grime
Trying to stretch the pound

An alley cat that's what you are
Running from shit heads and skin heads

You lick the white filth
Just to get the pound

Listen all economic exiles
Wage this revolution

Think of the land you left behind
Think of the biblical prodigal son

The voices of the prophets call
Now is the time to take heed

[Moto March 2000]

Derailed

It seems likely
The wheel will turn full circle

The crippling indebtedness
The stifling World Bank
The International Ministry of Finance

Through draconian misrule
Posterity has been mortgaged

Through warped priorities
The present is chained
The past is turned to waste

This is development-
One step forward
Two steps backwards

Look at the derailment

(Social Change September 1999) IMF derisively termed
International Ministry of Finance]

Their Lessons

Internecine strife
They create

Between and among us
Wedges, they drive

Dangling their stinking dollars
Pawns among us they nurture

Fratricide, matricide, patricide
They sow through their saboteurs

Dumping weapons of war on us
To boost their economies with arms trade

They teach us democracy
With guns, land mines, bombs, fighter planes

Take heed this is not a romantic view of us

[Social Change September 1999]

Concerned

Drowning in the sea
The sea of emptiness

Crippled by the tentacles
Tentacles of rootlessness

Wielding those penny certificates
Penny certificates no one has eyes for

Drenching and clouding minds
In liquor and cigarette smoke

On immorality existing
Trying to evade the consequences

I prescribe no solution
Hear the reverberations of the message

(Social Change September 1999)

Behind The Mask

Serpent
Dew-like promises
That's what they were
Waves of deception
Enveloped reality
That false bliss
Veiled the eyes
Serpent
Illusions
That kaleidoscopic glitter
Interred are those succulent songs
Dirges fill the air

[Ballads Of Our Lives 04.11.99]

No

Yet another farce
Yet another charade
Trying to hoodwink us
We refuse to be silenced
Listen to the toilet bowl
Flush down their pieces of paper

Leaving rats with our groundnuts
Leaving hyenas with our goats
Leaving the sacred cows with the alligators
That we can never do

Look and see their demise
The writing is on the wall
No one can hold back the time
We refuse to be taken hostage

[Moto December 1999]

Conscious

Refusing to be silenced
This is a mighty force
Preaching redemption
I will sing these songs
Their daggers, they sharpen
Their guns blaze
A prophet I am
Speaking messages they detest
I will sing these songs
Won't you help me sing these songs?

This is a sacrifice
Posterity will never forgive us

This is a sacrifice
The present cannot afford indifference

[Moto April 1999]

Modern Day Pharaoh

Uncle Sam
Get off my back
I am tired
The horse and rider game
You play at my peril
This my life
Is divine providence
I respect not your rule

To hell with your trouble brewing
Shameless hypocrite
I have no ears for your lessons
You teach fratricide
You are not a super power
You are the devil's power
Off to the gates of Hades
Blood sucking vampire
Remember Vietnam
Stop your games in Libya and Cuba
Let my people go Pharaoh

[Moto July 1999]

Celebration Time

Beat the drums
With maniacal zeal
Women ululate
Men let us hear
The shrill of your whistling
For we have graduated

No longer garden boys
But gardeners
No longer nannies
Domestic workers hear this
Domestic technicians

No longer master-servant
Shef-povo time, yes
Change is marching on
Do you hear that?

[Moto November 1998]

Inflammatory Speech

In his speech
The eerie hooting of an owl
The tentacles of thick darkness
The grotesque laugh of a hyena
The flutter of the wings of a hellish bat
The ominous stare of the night ape
That is the vampire I hear and see

The spattering of brains
Lacerating of human flesh
The works of pawns in the game
The hare-brained schemes must succeed
The world must be duped
What is this democracy all about?
Is the existence of an opposition an ailment?
Should the youths' hands be blood-stained?

(Moto November 1998)

Worker Power

This is the hour
For worker power
A rejection of extortion
That is the taproot of revolution

Impoverished bull terriers
Unleashed against the people
Rabbit tail like memories of the leaders
Arrogance is their hall mark

Rise my mighty people
Take the rhino by its horn
Sever the shackles and chains
Shoot down the rabid dogs

Dictators must go now
Down into the dustbins of history
This now is spring time
No one can hold back the season

[Moto March 1998 composed 09.12.97 room K12 Carr Saunders
Hall UZ]

Our Land

For the homeless
For the children
For our farmers
For our hills, valleys and plains
For the graves of our ancestors
For our own graves
For the hungry
For the thirsty
For our dances
Mbavarira, Mhande, Isitshikitsha,
Muchongoyo
For our monuments
For appeasing the angry slaughtered
For the repatriation
Of our kith and kin in the diaspora
For our freedom
Yes, this is our land

[Moto September 1997]

The Minotaurs

Sharp howling winds
Of masochism
On the television screen
The obliteration
Of humanity
This daemonic abyss

It gives them stiff erections
Oh the impotent
Trying to retrieve waning power
Playing noxious power games

Drinking human blood
Calling it wine
Sacrificing fellow beings
On the altar of vein glory
Devils masquerading as angels
See the obscenities

Setting in motion propaganda
Trying to mask reality
What about the orphans
What about the widows
Ominous floods of deception

Trying to plunge us
Into wintry darkness

I refuse to package my soul
In the thick foil of your deception
These thoughts will bolt burst

Posterity will know
Of your sadism
Of the fanning of strife
I will stand up and preach
For hope fast dissipates
Listen to the reverberations

[Moto May 1999]

Their Romp And Pomp

Alligators
The inflamed udder
Of the sacred cow
Village imps
The defiled village wells
The devil's advocates
Building the nation
Dams of liquor
Gouging out minds
Even the so-called soul' shepherds
At least could have been indifferent
Behind their romp and pomp
The resilience of our African norms and values

[Moto March 1999]

Stung

That blood drips
From their hands
Vongotumira vana kuhondo

Shameless propaganda
Floods our minds

Muchadura

The time for unmasking
Yes, it is now at hand

He died in a foreign land
A hot lead thorn in his heart

Listen to the wailing
Ominously gripping the nation
Vongotumira vana kuhondo
Onai vachadura

Listen to the heart rending wails
Of the widows
Robbed of their husbands

Listen to the wailing
Of the children
For their decapitated fathers

Oh mothers
Oh fathers

See the sacrificing of children
For the waning popularity

That blood drips
From their hands

Now we know the truth
Put millstones around their necks
Cast them into the darkest depths of the sea
Forever they shall dwell in the watery abyss

[Moto December 1998   *Vongotumira vana kuhondo*- sending children
to the war front. *Vachadura* –they shall reveal the truth]

A Battered Wife

You likened me to the seven wonders
The Seven Wonders of the World
This was when you almost went down
On your knees for my love
Promising me heaven on earth

Now you turn me into a punch bag
Do you now see beauty in black eyes and broken limbs?
Like dew in the sun
Your promises have vanished
Into hell on earth my life has turned
You dent our children's lives physically and psychologically
On us you vent your frustrations
Before your boss you have jelly in the knees

For your paltry pay packet, do not blame us
For the impending retrenchment, do not blame us
Do not make us victims of extended aggression
The demon in you, with reason, please exorcise
Or soon the fountain of my patience will run dry

(The Sunday News May 7, 1995)

Out Of Reach

Despondency soars
Like a bird of prey

In its steel talons
The shredded social fabric

Ignorance sinks its baobab tree like roots
Into this youthful nation
For schools have become a preserve for the few

Diseases multiply every minute
As hospital fees sky rocket
The cost of traditional medicines spirals out of reach

Basic necessities are now a luxury
Daily we are bombarded
By the **ever** escalating cost of living

News broadcasts petrify us
The sullen news reader's voice announces
'The price of … has gone up'

Our dented pride
There on the rubbish dump
Our Zimbabwe dollar is now the *Zimkwacha*
Continued over-taxation
Shriveling what little we earn

The gains of our liberation struggle

Submerge into the quicksand of disillusionment

Emotionally charged demonstrations
Degenerate into mindless riots
Trampling peace and justice

The stifling cost of living
Transforms begging into a national industry

The sun must shine again
Hope should sprout like new leaves in spring

[Employment and Training Opportunities September 1998]

On Tour

Then she took them
Took them
To the golden glimmer
Of the Sheraton

Took them
From the towering East Gate mall
To the West Gate sprawling maze

Then she laughed
When a child's voice asked
'Is this heaven?'

Then she took them
Took them
To the ramshackle shacks
Of Dzivaresekwa extension

Took them
To the damp, dark ghettoes
Of heaving Mbare and forgotten Epworth

Then this time her heart sank
When that voice quizzed
'Is this hell?'

[Social Change August 1998]

The Other Side

To them the poet
Is a singer of shallow praises

... empty platitudes
Where dirges would suffice

To them the poet
Is one choosing thick blindness

Seeing not mothers burying their children
Or the anguish on the factory floors

To them the poet
Sings all the correct songs

About the virtues of begging in the streets
Or the benevolence of donors
From another world

To them the poet perpetual
Is but an ape of the waBenzi culture

That clown on National days
Spewing slogans at us

The boulder of shame is on my shoulders

[Social Change August 1998]

Bolt Bursting

The poem of my protest
Is in a smudge of blood
On a graffiti laden wall
It is in sweat no longer trickling
Down an anger creased forehead

The poem of my protest
Is in a brick that will not be hurled
By my immobilized arm
It is in the echo of footsteps
No longer thudding the streets

The poem of my protest
Is in smouldering tear gas canisters
It is defiantly there
In the truncheon inflicted raw wounds
It is there in the bullet torn flesh
Now it must touch humanity
For justice and peace to prevail

[Social Change August 1998 awarded Diploma For Excellence
Scottish International Open Poetry Contest 1997]

Crystal and Smoke

Crystal strewn streets
Smouldering rubble
Spiky smell of drifting tear gas
Thick police presence
Is this a police state?

Truncheons abound
Automat Kalashnikovs
The liberator's gun
Now in the hands of the new oppressors
With the hares they ran
But hunted with the hounds

Bow out gracefully
For your place among the great
Rid yourself of sycophants
The waning popularity, retrieve
Peace time is up
Justice time is now

[Moto August 1998]

Dawn

When you whisper softly into my ear
When you crown me king
And I crown you queen of my soul
When I explore your soothing curves
When I thirst and hunger for you
When the fragrance of your natural perfume
Ensnares my sense of smell
When I am with you in that short lived dream
When we embrace like we will never let go
When we seem to surmount evil schemes
When I look at your perfectly sculptured features
When I speak of that mermaid
I enticed out of that other world
When I see that this is a house built on the sand
Tears flow profusely down my cheeks
Then illusions submerge into the quicksand of reality

[Mahogany January / February 1998]

Cost Of Freedom

Smile Edmund Burke
Your words, now they espouse
Keep them in the tentacles of darkness
Turn their revolution into an elusive dream
That is the new song they now sing
Sons and daughters of honest folk
Now will wallow in the muddy water of ignorance

The price to be paid for freedom soars
Maybe now is the time for real education
The honey moon of their brainwashing, soon will be over

Betrayal! Betrayal! A voice wails in the wilderness
Listen, Bob Marley
Would you their invitation, accept today
What of you, Ngugi Wa Thiong'o
Would you? Would you?
See they trample that which you taught
'Education for liberation'
That is the song of protest we have to sing
Like the Jericho walls these walls of ignorance must crumble

[Moto August 1992]

Recipe For Disaster

Ingredients: Thousands of the unemployed
Steel yoke taxation
          Socialist rhetoric coated full blown capitalism
          Charging – rhino-prices of everything
          Constricted former free thinkers
          Disgruntled students, peasants and workers
          Freedom fighters turned to squatters, beggars
          A home grown economic earthquake

Method: Put all these in a country in the third world
There is a hot dish of disaster before you.

[BWAZ BULLETIN NOVEMBER 1996]

To Onesimo Makani Kabweza

These are my tear drops
Tear drops on the page
The pages were your life
Onesimo Oh, Onesimo
Dust to dust, ashes to ashes
It had to be you this time
These inexplicable traffic accidents
Death- you baffle us mortals

[Moto June 1993]

To God

As I tread through this land
Teach me to be light
Where there is darkness
Teach me to sow love
Where hate abounds
Teach me to forgive and to forget
Where revenge yearns to surface
For in Sicily they say revenge is a season in hell
Teach me to cage my tongue
When evil words threaten to bolt burst
Teach me to be a harbinger of hope
Where despair engulfs humanity
Teach me to promote unity
Where disunity rears its ugly head
Teach me not to be discordant
Where the sweet sound of harmony prevails
Teach me to promulgate the sanctity of life
Where the law of the jungle takes precedence
Teach me to be the light house
For many a ship lost at sea
Teach me to help the helpless and the weak
Teach me to be incorruptible
Where quick riches entice
Teach me to stay away from Delilah
For it is said beauty is a witch
And that destruction walks with smiling faces
Teach me to realize that you are my health and strength
Teach me to humble myself
For it is said wisdom is found in the simplest of places
Teach me to be just
To realize that injustice brings forth retrogression

And is a threat to civilization
Above all teach me to know you
In times of plenty and in times of want
Also teach me to be an embodiment
Of all that you have taught
All you have taught since the beginning of time

[Moto February 1999 composed 06.06.95]

Veiled Eyes

Having gobbled the diet
The diet of befuddling religions
Having swallowed hook, line and sinker
The gospel of apostasy
Now with their warped minds
They denigrate themselves unwittingly
Enveloped by the darkness of foolishness

The essence of our ways is warped
Labelling our ways, ancestral worship
Conveniently forgetting our intercessors
Hacking at the roots of our confidence
Defiling all our sacrosanct shrines
But the resilience is plain to see

[oneghanaonevoice]

African Drum

The demonized drum
Speaks to my soul
Soothing my African soul
Sweetly caressing it

Invoking those spirits
The restless spirits of my people
Hot iron branded pagan
Those that dangled at noose ends

Reverberations of the drum
Spelling out my happiness
At times messages of strife
The demonized drum

[oneghanaonevoice]

To Dennis Brutus

In the beginning was the word
In the end will be the word
For you used words to confront
Confronting those truncheons
Confronting the racist jackboots
For yours was righteous indignation

Posterity will treasure the words
The struggle is not yet over
Greed pollutes our planet
There are the old and new foes
Your words will be our compass

Did you leave poetic attacks on xenophobia
The reversal of the gains of the struggle
You must have shed a tear or two
Somewhere on the pages must be teardrops
The activist in you did not die
The immortality lies in the works

[oneghanaonevoice]

Erasing My Memories

Mutabaruka then, you moved me
To take up arms against apartheid
The killings in Soweto, in Sharpeville
The bombing of exiles in Zimbabwe
The bombings in Mozambique
The bombings in Zambia and elsewhere

Peter Tosh you moved me to tears
Moved me to fight against apartheid
That callous jailing of Nelson Mandela
The hanging of little talked of Benjamin Moloise
The mysterious death of Steve Bantu Biko
The deaths of all heroic sons and daughters

How can I forget Dennis Brutus
Choose to forget Ruth First
Choose to forget Umkhonto We Sizwe
Separate me from that African struggle
That African struggle for freedom

Those so-called attacks on foreigners
The smell of burning human flesh
Those all too familiar photos
The infamous necklacing of fellow victims
Fellow victims of poverty, ignorance and disease

The shocking violence on fellow Africans
The displacement of fellow Africans
Europe dismantles her borders
We slavishly cling to colonial legacies

Who alienates me from my struggle?
Who seeks to erase my memories?

French Conference in the DRC

Laugh your lungs out
But that is where we are
Not a fatalistic acceptance
A backhander from reality

Then it got to the marrow
This poem is part of the evidence
Dreaming no longer in my mother tongue
Perhaps now a cultural bat

Still in the spider's web
The entanglement gets deeper
Now that was total surrender
Celebrating growth of the French language

Against the backdrop of abject poverty
In the background of foreign gunfire
A French conference in the jungles of Africa
This is an avalanche of questions

[oneghanaonevoice]

Dambudzo

Troubling the racist Rhodesian system
That one man demonstration
Little David against Goliath
Trouble in faculty corridors
From the university of Rhodesia to Oxford
Pursuing prancing poetry and prose

Troubling them at the Guardian fiction prize function
Troubling those that could not cross
The racial divide in matters of the heart
Troubling the greedy and the corrupt
Seeing the revolution derailed
Were you trouble, Dambudzo

With those allusions to Greek mythology
Still troubling us in symposiums
The person that became the poetry
That immortality long secured
Dambudzo you cannot be remembered
That is the beauty of your art

[oneghanaonevoice]

Africa Day Reflections

Behind it all
Our unmistakable resilience

The abundance of hope
For we are no pessimists

The reality plain to see
Africa bleeding profusely

Fires of discord fanned
The beneficiaries in glee

Robbed of childhood
Playing fields bereft of children

High on lsd, heroin, mandrax
Raping, robbing, killing with impunity

The hidden hand at it
Propping unpopular regimes

The ever widening chasms
Bickering over foreign ideas

Africa bleeding profusely
Somewhere they drink blood

The prophets long said it
The richest place, home to the poorest race

In Somalia, in Sudan, Ethiopia
Everywhere the bloody feuding

The scramble for blood diamonds
Everywhere death and destruction

Beneath this desolation
The undying hope sprouting

[oneghanaonevoice]

Old New Song

This song is new
For this song is old
This song has been sung before
This song shall always be sung
This song shall be about freedom
It has always been about freedom
This song shall be a memorial
This song shall be a compass
Never shall we forget its roots
Never shall we forget its timeless message

This song shall be sung off key
For it defies those categories
The song is the future built today
Firmly rooted on the foundation of the past
This song shall drive them crazy
Those armed with opportunistic tendencies
The gluttons riding on our backs
The parasites sucking our blood dry

Won't you help me sing this song
In the discordant voice lies the melody
This song is the rattling of old bones
The old bones that gave us direction
Those old bones that shall always have life

This song shall speak of the heroes
Those that have not been defiled by lies
It shall bear the true story of our people

This shall be etched on our minds
There, in the heroes acre of our minds
There, where Patrick Kombayi lives
There, where Ndabaningi Sithole lives
There, where Jairos Jiri forever lives
There, where many unsung heroes live
There, where new heroes are defined

This song shall live forever
Though it may sound discordant to some
This song shall speak of liberty
This song shall speak of the future
It shall not be sung by demigods
This song shall be against polarization
This song is a part of the continental anthem
It is a part of all freedom fighters' anthems
It shall be a song of all yearning for freedom
They shall sing it in Palestine against evil
They shall sing it where oppression refuses to die
Won't you help me sing this song?

Wilting

The flower is wilting
Lies parched and shrivelled
The future destined for the morgue
While the gluttons thrive

The jobs daily exported
The offshore accounts fattened
The self aggrandisement race is on
Platinum, gold, diamonds... gone

The future in the throes of death
Submerged by ways of unemployment
Seeking solace in mind bending substances
Codeine, cocaine, ...killing the future

Back In The Fire

The hopes are dashed
Driven by forces of brutality
The grinding squalor back home
Driven into crocodile bellies
Fleeing from crocodiles at home
Those that have an iron fist

Driven into crocodiles' mouths
Dreams of Egoli submerged
Families in anticipation waiting
Waiting, waiting and oblivious of it all
That dad died trying to fend for them
That mum became a meal for crocodiles

What is the source of these miscreants
Bereft of any sympathy, lacking empathy
What is the root of this obscene kleptomania
That stashes national wealth abroad
Investing in Dubai, Singapore, Switzerland
While floods of poverty drown the nation

Serving Gods

With the truncheon
Named the black swine
You bash the skulls
Fracture the limbs
Extirpate the lives

With the paltry pay packet
There in your torn pocket
You prop unpopular thieves
Propping regimes from hell
While submerged in squalor

To a pulp bashing fellow sufferers
The day of reckoning is dawning
You shall be weighed in the balance
There you shall be found wanting
No more will you quench that thirst
That thirst for innocent blood

Addicts

Babies strapped to their backs
Some rolling about in the dust
Mothers' minds hoping, expectant
Fathers hoping, hoping for a win

Endless trips to fortune tellers
Interpretations attached to dreams
Dreams reduced to torn betting forms
Hope refusing to be interred
Always the big one that got away

The addiction then sets in firmly
Hope for rehabilitation fast dissipating
The betting drug akin to crystal meth
On the horizon the looming catastrophe

Objects Of Pity

Bereft of empathy
Emptied of ubuntu
By years of deprivation
Weeds of squalor there
There in poverty stricken minds

Fighting over the crumbs
Yet the multinationals suck
Suck the African resources dry
Oblivious of Anglo-American schemes
Oblivious of Chinese encroachment

Minds befuddled by drugs
Weird feelings of superiority
Engaging in ominous self hate
Blind to the colour of the economy
Blind to the root cause of squalor
The sprawling shacks everywhere
Hands dripping with African blood

Trashing the ideals of ubuntu
Fragmenting that unity forged
In the crucible of racial discrimination
Forgetting about places of refuge
North of the Vhembe river and beyond

The shame of it plain to see
The damascene moment on the horizon

Grim Necessity

Driven by grim necessity
That great mind long said it
Driven not by ignorance
Driven by the need for survival
Not driven by obduracy

Driven by gnawing hunger
By the grinding poverty
Driven by the house of hunger
Into the hands of brutality
Acrid cordite now inhaling

Those unthinking hounds
Blindingly following orders
Thrashing the poor like corn
Pleasing those with full pantries
The point of no return looming

Mmap New African Poets Series

If you have enjoyed *Along the Way*, consider these other fine books in the **New African Poets Series** from *Mwanaka Media and Publishing*:

I Threw a Star in a Wine Glass by Fethi Sassi
Best New African Poets 2017 Anthology by Tendai R Mwanaka and Daniel Da Purificacao
Logbook Written by a Drifter by Tendai Rinos Mwanaka
Mad Bob Republic: Bloodlines, Bile and a Crying Child by Tendai Rinos Mwanaka
Zimbolicious Poetry Vol 1 by Tendai R Mwanaka and Edward Dzonze
Zimbolicious Poetry Vol 2 by Tendai R Mwanaka and Edward Dzonze
Zimbolicious: An Anthology of Zimbabwean Literature and Arts, Vol 3 by Tendai Mwanaka
Under The Steel Yoke by Jabulani Mzinyathi
Fly in a Beehive by Thato Tshukudu
Bounding for Light by Richard Mbuthia
Sentiments by Jackson Matimba
Best New African Poets 2018 Anthology by Tendai R Mwanaka and Nsah Mala
Words That Matter by Gerry Sikazwe
The Ungendered by Delia Watterson
Ghetto Symphony by Mandla Mavolwane
Sky for a Foreign Bird by Fethi Sassi
A Portrait of Defiance by Tendai Rinos Mwanaka
Zimbolicious: An Anthology of Zimbabwean Literature and Arts, Vol 4 by Tendai Mwanaka and Jabulani Mzinyathi
When Escape Becomes the only Lover by Tendai R Mwanaka
ويَسهَرُ اللَّيلُ عَلَى شَفَتي...وَالغَمَام by Fethi Sassi
A Letter to the President by Mbizo Chirasha
This is not a poem by Richard Inya

94

Pressed flowers by John Eppel

Righteous Indignation by Jabulani Mzinyathi:

Blooming Cactus by Mikateko Mbambo

Rhythm of Life by Olivia Ngozi Osouha

Travellers Gather Dust and Lust by Gabriel Awuah Mainoo

Chitungwiza Mushamukuru: An Anthology from Zimbabwe's Biggest Ghetto Town by Tendai Rinos Mwanaka

Zimbolicious: An Anthology of Zimbabwean Literature and Arts, Vol 5 by Tendai Mwanaka

Because Sadness is Beautiful? by Tanaka Chidora

Of Fresh Bloom and Smoke by Abigail George

Shades of Black by Edward Dzonze

Best New African Poets 2020 Anthology by Tendai Rinos Mwanaka, Lorna Telma Zita and Balddine Moussa

This Body is an Empty Vessel by Beaton Galafa

Between Places by Tendai Rinos Mwanaka

Best New African Poets 2021 Anthology by Tendai Rinos Mwanaka, Lorna Telma Zita and Balddine Moussa

Zimbolicious: An Anthology of Zimbabwean Literature and Arts, Vol 6 by Tendai Mwanaka and Chenjerai Mhondera

A Matter of Inclusion by Chad Norman

Keeping the Sun Secret by Mariel Awendit

سِجلٌ مَكتُوبٌ لِثَانِه by Tendai Rinos Mwanaka

Ghetto Blues by Tendai Rinos Mwanaka

Zimbolicious: An Anthology of Zimbabwean Literature and Arts, Vol 7 by Tendai Rinos Mwanaka and Tanaka Chidora

Best New African Poets 2022 Anthology by Tendai Rinos Mwanaka and Helder Simbad

Dark Lines of History by Sithembele Isaac Xhegwana

Soon to be released

a sky is falling by Nica Cornell
The politics of Life by Mandhla Mavolwane
Death of a Statue by Samuel Chuma
Strides of Hope by Tawanda Chigavazira

https://facebook.com/MwanakaMediaAndPublishing/

Printed in the United States
by Baker & Taylor Publisher Services